BBC TopGear DOT-TO-DOT

KEVIN PETTMAN

ILLUSTRATIONS BY
THE COMIC STRIPPER

THE BEST ~~BOOK~~ *Dot-to-Dot* BOOK IN THE WORLD!

BBC
BOOKS

CONTENTS

Actually, ignore the above safety warning. Doing a dot-to-dot is incredibly easy (unless you're The Stig – some say his brain only works in binary code) and we added that caution to make this book seem more exhilarating than it really is. Sorry. But believe us, the dot-to-dot is making a BIG comeback, so *Top Gear* has hitched a lift with it and sketched a lorry-load of half-finished pictures and laughs for you to fill in.

Jeremy's
~~IDIOT'S~~ GUIDE TO DOT-TO-DOT

1. Pick up a pencil/pen/crayon
2. Look for the black dot with number one next to it.
3. Put pencil/pen/crayon on the dot next to number one.
4. Draw a line from number one to number two, then number three, four, five etc.
5. If you see a ★ next to a number, this means you lift your pencil/pen/crayon OFF the page and restart at the next numbered dot.
6. Join all the dots up to complete the picture.

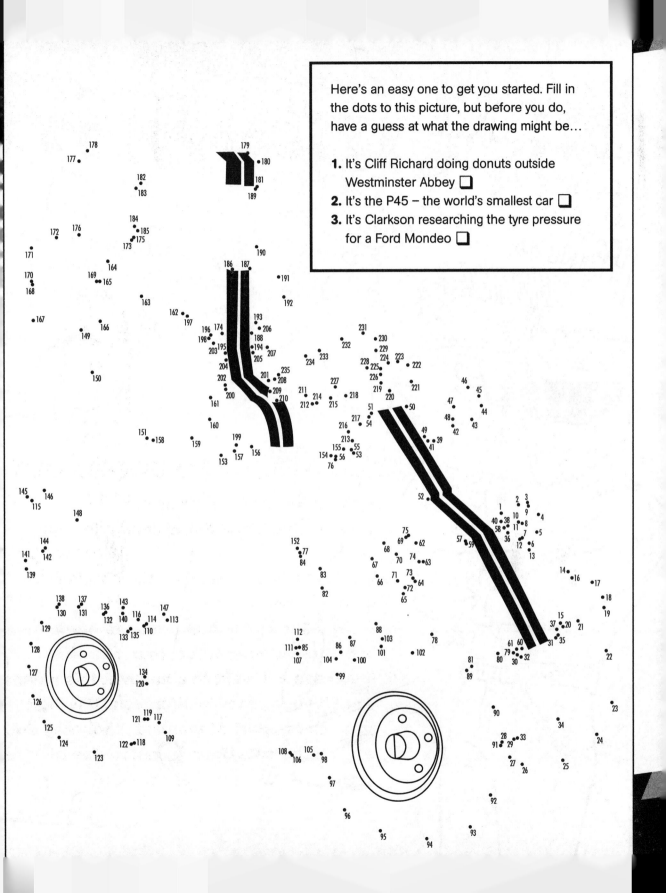

Here's an easy one to get you started. Fill in the dots to this picture, but before you do, have a guess at what the drawing might be...

1. It's Cliff Richard doing donuts outside Westminster Abbey ☐

2. It's the P45 – the world's smallest car ☐

3. It's Clarkson researching the tyre pressure for a Ford Mondeo ☐

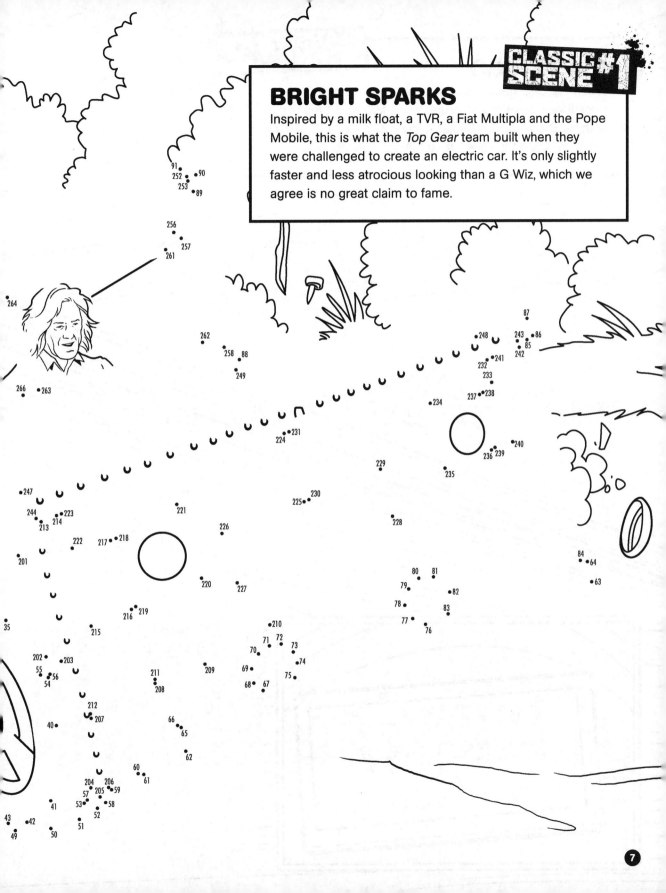

BRIGHT SPARKS

Inspired by a milk float, a TVR, a Fiat Multipla and the Pope Mobile, this is what the *Top Gear* team built when they were challenged to create an electric car. It's only slightly faster and less atrocious looking than a G Wiz, which we agree is no great claim to fame.

CAPTAIN GO

When *Top Gear* needed someone to max out the 1,000hp Bugatti Veyron, we're pretty sure James May wasn't top of their wish list. But fair play to Captain Slow – he gave it the beans to reach an insane top speed. It was all just a blur for him.

DOT HAPPENS NEXT?

Always expect the unexpected to happen on *Top Gear*. On second thoughts, expect the expected cock-up to always happen on *Top Gear*. Here we have Jeremy on a campsite, lovingly preparing an evening meal for his *Top Gear* comrades. What could possibly happen next? Fill in the dots, then turn the page.

THIS IS DOT HAPPENS NEXT!

Oh well, at least Jeremy's idiotic behaviour brought the camping weekend to a swift halt. Although, the agony went on as the guys had to drive home in a Kia Cerato. We're still trying to work out which scenario is more embarrassing.

RUN AWAY!

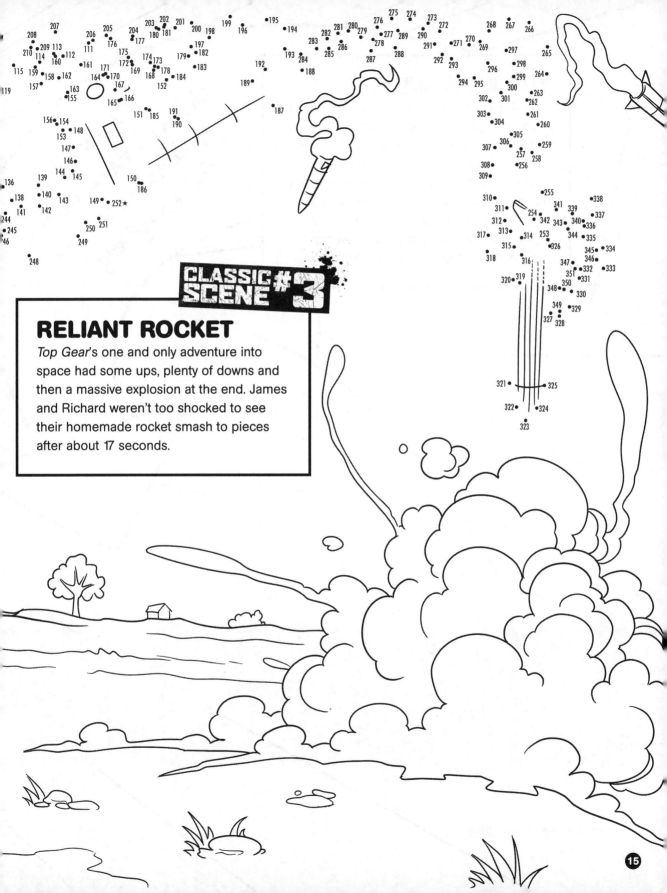

CLASSIC SCENE #3

RELIANT ROCKET

Top Gear's one and only adventure into space had some ups, plenty of downs and then a massive explosion at the end. James and Richard weren't too shocked to see their homemade rocket smash to pieces after about 17 seconds.

THE ALFA MALE

Cool. Precise. Sophisticated. Clever. These are the things Jeremy Clarkson might like us to describe him as. Loud, oafish, slapdash and irritating are the words Richard and James would probably use. Nonetheless, Jeremy is a true petrolhead – just think of him as an alpha male in an Alfa Romeo, with the mission of setting the world free from safety cameras, traffic wardens and Vauxhall Vectras.

Check out Jeremy's favourite tool. He likes to use it to fix * everything.

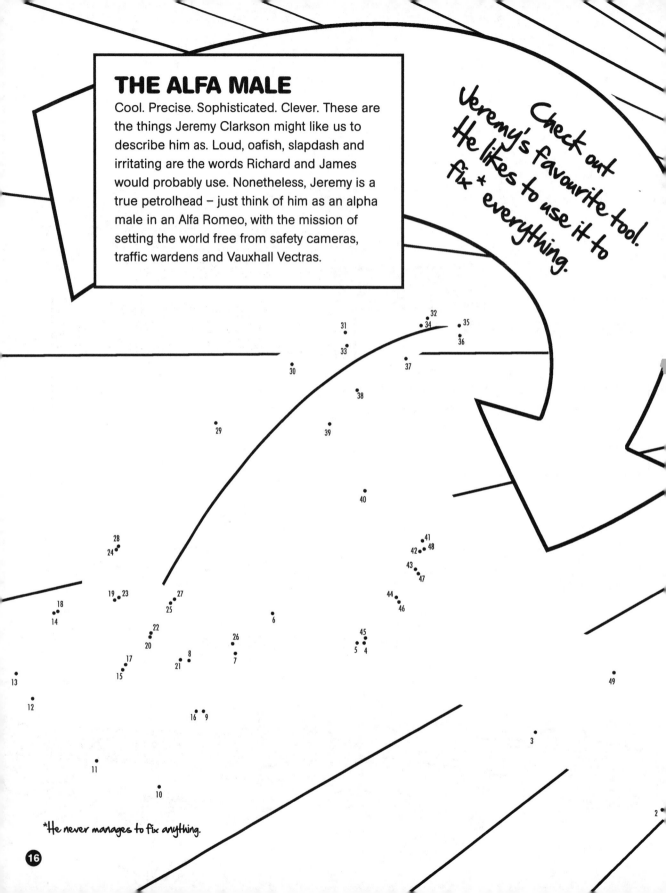

*He never manages to fix anything.

ENGLAND

DOVER

COASTING IT

The *Top Gear* boys were challenged to take four-wheeled floaters 24 miles across the Channel to France. Hammond and May abandoned their 'ships' in Dover, so Jezza did a very un-*Top Gear* thing and scooped them up to charge across the waves. It worked – the guys became the first people with British passports to be overjoyed at setting foot in Sangatte. Join all the dots to complete Clarkson's Nissank sea creature.

● SANGATTE

FRANCE

RICHARD HAIR-MOND

Top Gear's telly life spans well into double digits, and over this time lots of things have changed – including Richard Hammond's well-coiffed hair. Now's your big chance to play barber shop and recreate his various styles, plus a hat-trick of other fine head garments.

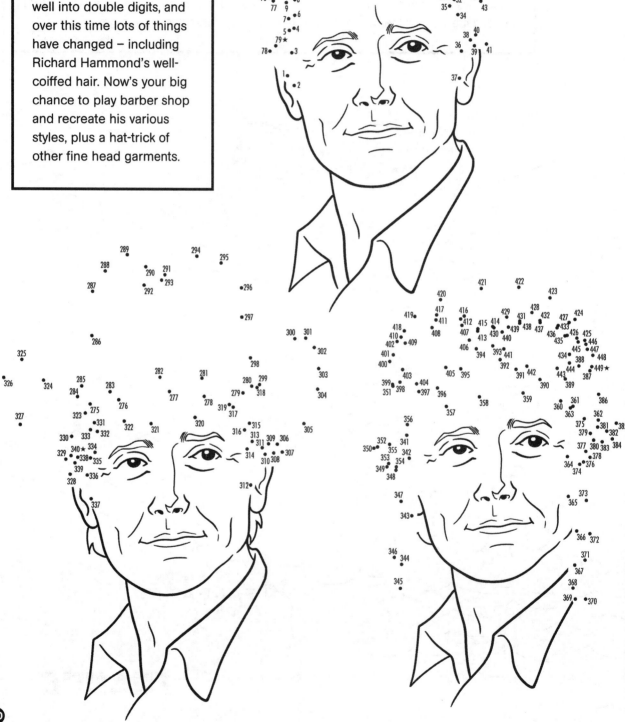

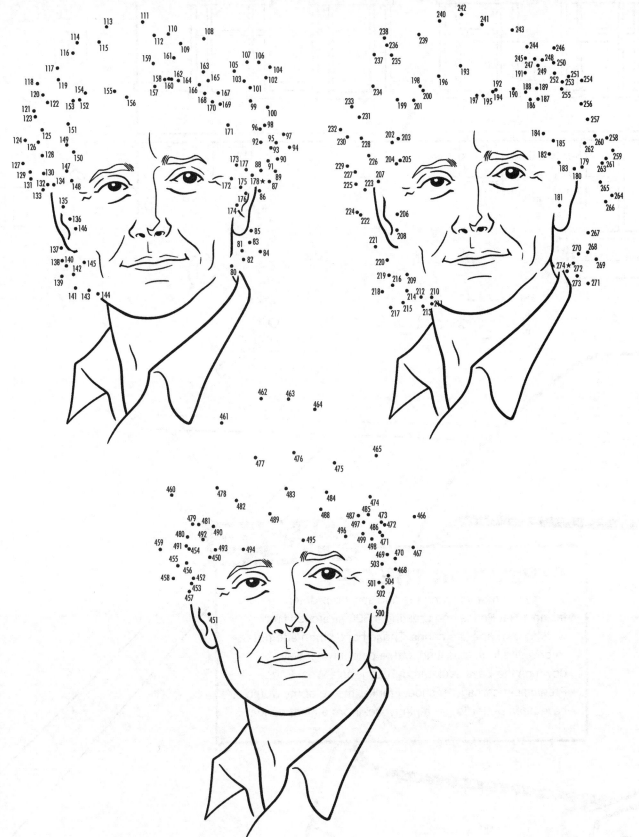

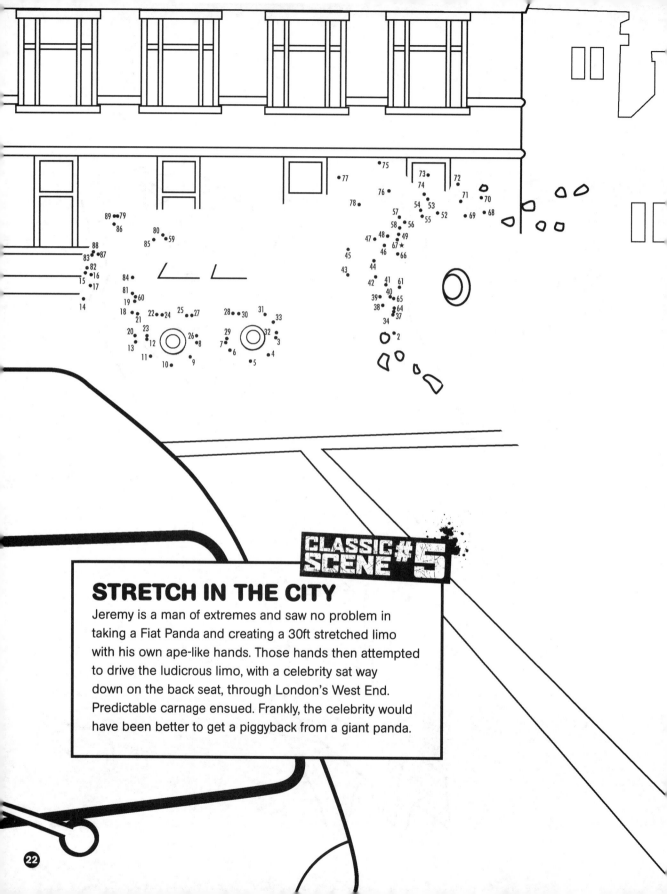

STRETCH IN THE CITY

Jeremy is a man of extremes and saw no problem in taking a Fiat Panda and creating a 30ft stretched limo with his own ape-like hands. Those hands then attempted to drive the ludicrous limo, with a celebrity sat way down on the back seat, through London's West End. Predictable carnage ensued. Frankly, the celebrity would have been better to get a piggyback from a giant panda.

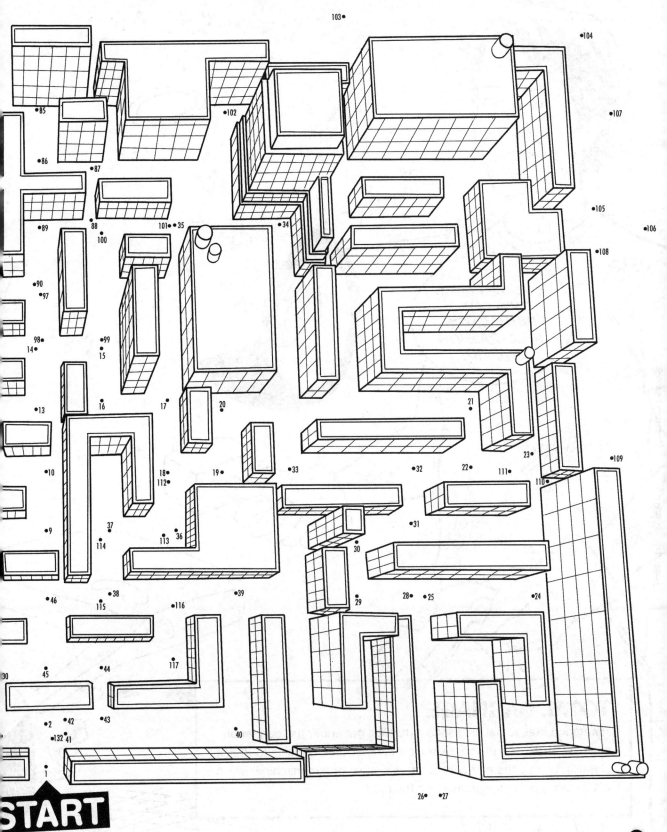

START

•133

TOTAL CARNAGE

Hammond likes to get his hands dirty. He'll get under the bonnet of anything from Land Rovers to muscle cars, Bowler Wildcats to British classics. Link up the numbers to see his latest dream machine, which will certainly prove a nightmare on the road.

CLASSIC SCENE #6

MOTORHOME MADNESS

After their previous attempt at a camping weekend went without a hitch (flick back to page 12), the guys are challenged to go camping again. This time, they have to adapt their vehicles as multipurpose cars/campervans. Jeremy's big idea towered above the rest.

29

LOOK AFTER NUMBER 2

When you're driving to the North Pole, you must look after and protect your co-driver. He's the guy who could save you from a polar bear, rescue you from a glacier and, er, stand guard as you do your daily business off the back of the truck. Draw in the dots to reveal the lengths James goes to just so Jeremy can do his job.

JAMES, ARE YOU SHOWING OFF OR ARE YOU ACTUALLY LOOKING FOR *BEARS* OVER THERE?

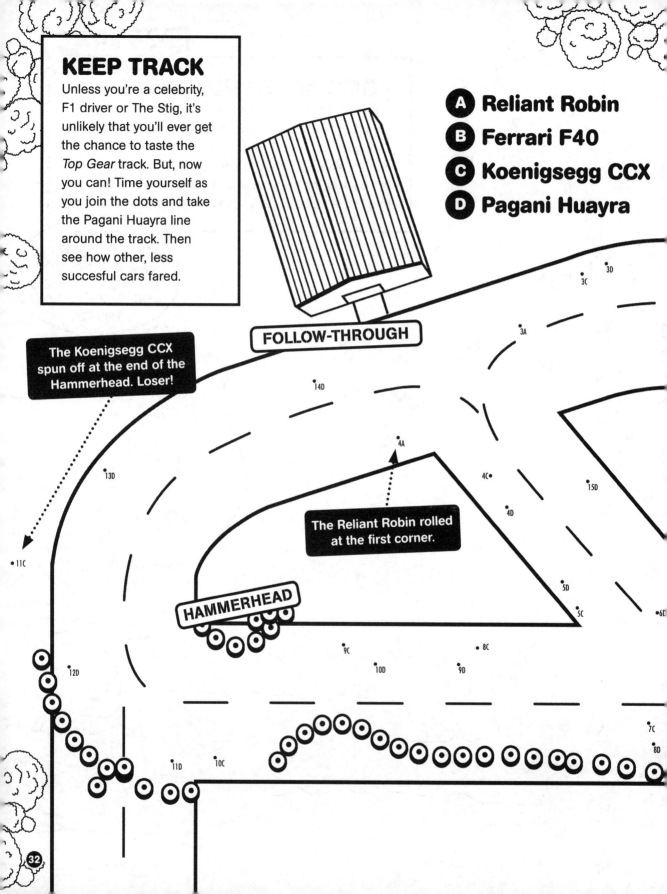

KEEP TRACK

Unless you're a celebrity, F1 driver or The Stig, it's unlikely that you'll ever get the chance to taste the *Top Gear* track. But, now you can! Time yourself as you join the dots and take the Pagani Huayra line around the track. Then see how other, less succesful cars fared.

A Reliant Robin
B Ferrari F40
C Koenigsegg CCX
D Pagani Huayra

The Koenigsegg CCX spun off at the end of the Hammerhead. Loser!

FOLLOW-THROUGH

The Reliant Robin rolled at the first corner.

HAMMERHEAD

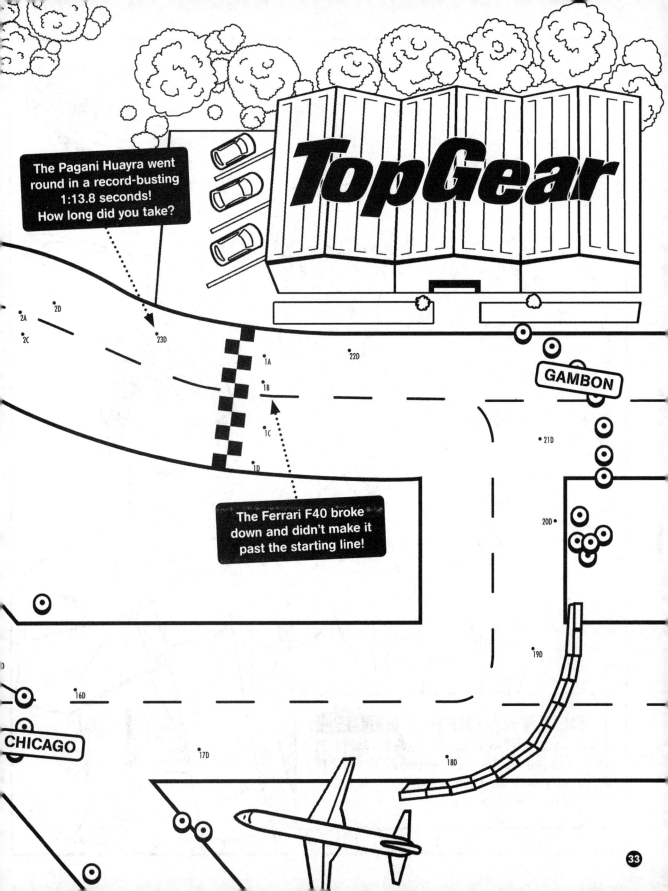

DOT THE DIFFERENCE

James Steed, Roger St. Hammond and Jason Clarkson are… The Interceptors! Fill in the dots to the picture on the right and see if you can spot the subtle differences.

MOTOR MOUTH

CLASSIC SCENE #8

This is a very special *Top Gear* moment, ladies and gents. When you've completed this dot to dot of Jeremy blasting the Ariel Atom round the track, you'll witness a rare occasion of him having nothing to say for himself.

IT'S ALL PART OF THE ADVENTURE OF CARAVANNING.

MAP

FULL OF HOT AIR

Just like the kid at school whose ears you'd flick, does *Top Gear*'s continual tinkering with caravans mean they are, secretly, in love with them? Here, James' pilot's license becomes very handy as he takes this love/hate relationship to ridiculous new heights. Back on terra firma, Richard tries to offer him a sense of direction.

TOP GEAR MATHS

Top Gear has never been that hot with maths. But not to worry because for this test we've been given the answers already! Choose from the five answers listed and fill in on the dotted line. After you've filled in the dot to dots first, of course.

INDIA CHALLENGE

CAMPING CHALLENGE

NORTH POLE CHALLENGE

VIETNAM CHALLENGE

DEEP SOUTH CHALLENGE

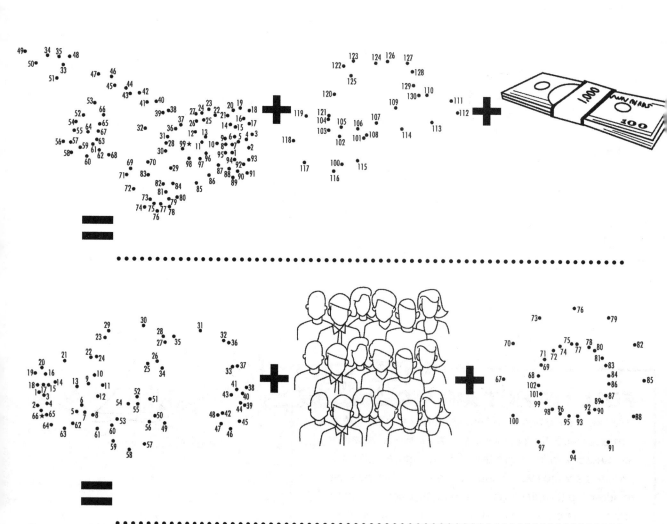

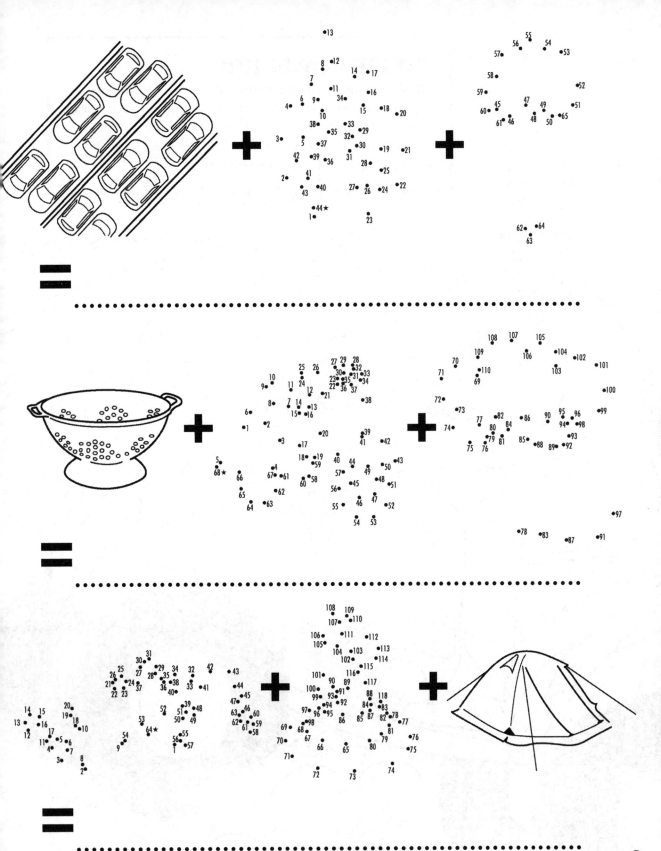

41

HORSE POWERRR!

When it comes to charging through the British countryside, *Top Gear* will go to any lengths. Jezza will jump on a quad bike, small off-roader or even a souped-up mobility scooter. And after you've put pen to paper here, you'll see that Hammond loves having a bit of horse power under him.

GUESS WHO?

The objects on the left are some of the things that make one of the *Top Gear* presenters very happy. Link up all the dots to create the chap in question.

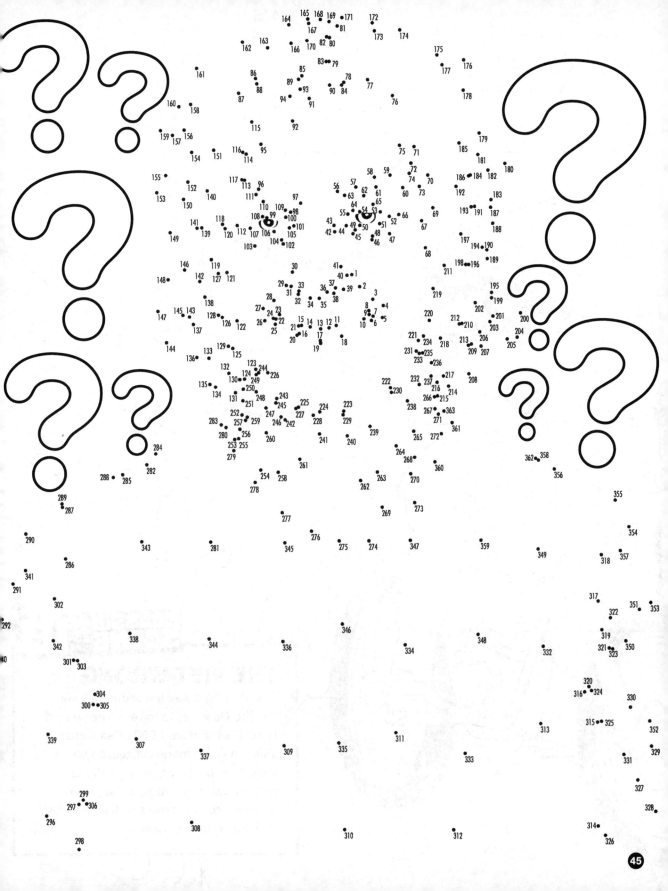

45

CLASSIC
SCENE #10

THE VIET-WRONG

There's a right way, the wrong way and
the *Top Gear* way to travel a foreign land.
Here, the trio drive 1,000 miles across
Vietnam in the monsoon season on
knackered old bikes, wearing stupid
clothes, carrying ludicrous cargo and
wearing kitchen utensils as helmets. Yes
sir – that's the *Top Gear* way.

47

THE STIG'S GERMAN COUSIN

THE STIG'S CHINESE COUSIN

THE STIG'S AFRICAN COUSIN

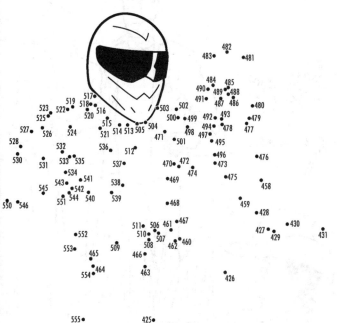

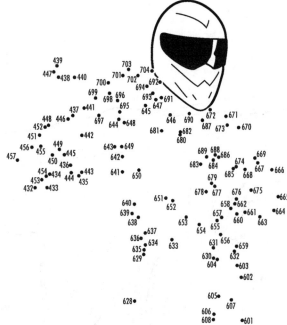

WE. ARE. FAMILY…

…I've got all my sisters with me.
Ahem, that's not true as The Stig
doesn't have any sisters, we don't
think, but we guaranteed the publisher
we'd get at least one Sister Sledge
gag in this book. When you've joined
up all the dots, you'll have drawn all of
The Stig's relatives. Now all you need
to do is draw a line from each Stig to
'its' name.

THE STIG'S ITALIAN COUSIN

THE STIG'S AMERICAN COUSIN

CLASSIC #11
SCENE

SANK YOU

Why is Hammond flapping about in a lake in Botswana, shouting 'Oliver!' while his undercrackers get wetter than Tom Daley's speedos? Is Oliver the name of the water buffalo he's wrestling? Or maybe it's his scuba diving instructor? Join all the dots to reveal what's going on.

DEEP TROUBLE

Driving across the deep south of America, there are rules to adhere to. But as we know, the *Top Gear* rules transcend all borders – even if that risks having to taste the local knuckle sandwich and baseball bat pie. Jeremy's homemade paintwork caused some serious disturbance to the locals.

SOME SAY...

Top Gear's Tame Racing Driver likes to do his talking out on the track, or not, if you know what we mean. But that's not to say he doesn't have the odd thought now and then. Complete the dots, then draw in what his Stigness could possibly be thinking about here.

CAN'T SEE THE AP-PEEL

Small, compact, unnoticeable. Not words often used in the same sentence as 'Jeremy' and 'Clarkson'. But when Jeremy Clarkson arrives at the BBC for another mind-numbing meeting, this time he was small, compact and strangely unnoticeable.

CLASSIC SCENE #13

46
45
44
43
189
190
191
42
41 197 192 184
193 183
40 198 196
199 195 194 210 183
200
39
37 205
38 30
29
28
27
26
25
24

57

DOT-TO-DOT YOURSELF

Look, it's nearly the end of the book and, quite frankly, we've hit rock bottom on the dot-to-dot ideas front. But you've had plenty of practice by now, so it's about time you pulled your finger out. Just draw a big object (how about a car?) in pencil, then number lots of dots on it and finally rub out all the lines. Now you're ready to join all the dots again. It could be the best DIY project ever connected with *Top Gear*.

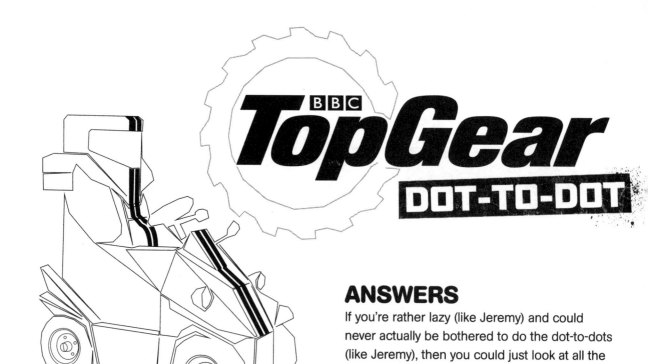

BBC TopGear
DOT-TO-DOT

ANSWERS

If you're rather lazy (like Jeremy) and could never actually be bothered to do the dot-to-dots (like Jeremy), then you could just look at all the lovely complete pictures here. It's cheating in a way, but Jeremy won't worry about that.

Pages 6-7

Pages 8-9

Pages 10-11

Pages 12-13

Pages 14-15

Pages 16-17

Pages 18-19

Pages 20-21

Pages 22-23

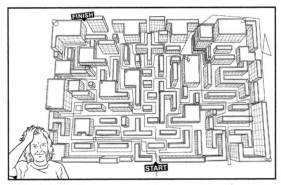

Pages 24-25

Pages 26-27

Pages 28-29

Pages 30-31

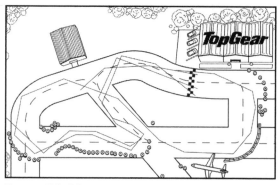

Pages 32-33

Pages 34-35

Pages 36-37

Pages 38-39

= Camping Challenge

= Deep South Challenge

= Vietnam Challenge

= India Challenge

= North Pole Challenge

Pages 40-41

Pages 42-43

Pages 44-45

Pages 46-47

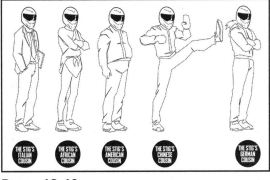

Pages 48-49

Pages 50-51

Pages 52-53

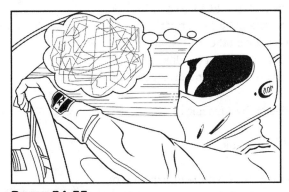

Pages 54-55

Pages 56-57

AND ON THAT BOMBSHELL...

That's it – you've journeyed through the action-packed world of *Top Gear* dot-to-dots and reached the last page! Well, there is the page at the back saying something about ISBN and how trees make paper, but not even James May is interested in that stuff.

1 3 5 7 9 10 8 6 4 2

Ebury Publishing
Random House, 20 Vauxhall Bridge Road,
London, SW1V 2SA

A Penguin Random House Company

Addresses for companies within Penguin Random House can be found at:
global.penguinrandomhouse.com

Project management and design by Amazing15

www.eburypublishing.co.uk

A CIP catalogue record for this book is available from the British Library

ISBN 9781849908535

Printed and bound by CPI Group (UK) Ltd, Croydon, CR0 4YY

Penguin Random House is committed to a sustainable future for
our business, our readers and our planet. This book is made from
Forest Stewardship Council® certified paper.

MIX
Paper from
responsible sources
FSC® C019777